21 Moral Essays From Francis Bacon

Condensed from

The Essays or Counsels, Civil and Moral, of Francis Ld. Verulam Viscount St. Albans

Presented by Don Guzz

I0438430

Biography of Sir Bacon

* Francis Bacon, 1st Viscount St Albans,[1] KC (22 January 1561 – 9 April 1626) was an English philosopher, statesman, scientist, lawyer, jurist, author and pioneer of the scientific method. He served both as Attorney General and Lord Chancellor of England. Bacon has been called the creator of empiricism.[2] His works established and popularised inductive methodologies for scientific inquiry, often called the Baconian method, or simply the scientific method. His demand for a planned procedure of investigating all things natural marked a new turn in the rhetorical and theoretical framework for science, much of which still surrounds conceptions of proper methodology today. His dedication probably led to his death, bringing him into a rare historical group of scientists who were killed by their own experiments.

* Bacon was knighted in 1603, and created both the Baron Verulam in 1618, and the Viscount St Alban in 1621;[3] as he died without heirs both peerages became extinct upon his death. He famously died of pneumonia contracted while studying the effects of freezing on the preservation of meat.

* Early life

Bacon was born on 22 January 1561 at York House near the Strand in London, the son of Sir Nicholas Bacon by his second wife Anne (Cooke) Bacon, the daughter of noted humanist Anthony Cooke. His mother's sister was married to William Cecil, 1st Baron Burghley, making Burghley Francis Bacon's uncle. Biographers believe that Bacon was educated at home in his early years owing to poor health (which plagued him throughout his life), receiving tuition from John Walsall, a graduate of Oxford with a strong leaning towards Puritanism. He entered Trinity College, Cambridge, on 5 April 1573 at the age of twelve,[4] living for three years there together with his older brother Anthony under the personal tutelage of Dr John Whitgift, future Archbishop of Canterbury.]

Moral 1: Of Truth

WHAT is truth? said jesting Pilate,and would not stay for an answer. Certainly there be, that delight in giddiness, and count it a bondage to fix a belief; affecting free-will in thinking, as well as in acting. And though the sects of philosophers of that kind be gone, yet there remain certain discoursing wits, which are of the same veins, though there be not so much blood in them, as was in those of the ancients. But it is not only the difficulty and labor, which men take in finding out of truth, nor again, that when it is found, it imposes upon men's thoughts, that doth bring lies in favor; but a natural, though corrupt love, of the lie itself. One of the later school of the Grecians, examines the matter, and is at a stand, to think what should be in it, that men should love lies; where neither they make for pleasure, as with poets, nor for advantage, as with the merchant; but for the lie's sake. But I cannot tell; this same truth, is a naked, and open day-light, that doth not show the masks, and mummeries, and triumphs, of the world, half so stately and daintily as candle-lights. Truth may perhaps come to the price of a pearl, that shows best by day; but it will not rise to the price of a diamond, or carbuncle, that shows best in varied lights. A mixture of a lie doth ever add pleasure. Doth any man doubt, that if there were taken out of men's minds, vain opinions, flattering hopes, false valuations, imaginations as one would, and the like, but it would leave the minds, of a number of men, poor shrunken things, full of melancholy and indisposition, and unpleasing to themselves?

One of the fathers, in great severity, called poesy vinum daemonum, because it fires the imagination; and yet, it is but with the shadow of a lie. But it is not the lie that passes through the mind, but the lie that sinks in, and settles in it, that doth the hurt; such as we spake of before. But howsoever these things are thus in men's depraved judgments, and affections, yet truth, which only doth judge itself, teachs that the inquiry of truth, which is the love-making, or wooing of it, the knowledge of truth, which is the presence of it, and the belief of truth, which is the enjoying of it, is the sovereign good of human nature. The first creature of God, in the works of the days, was the light of the sense; the last, was the light of reason; and his sabbath work ever since, is the illumination of his Spirit. First he breathed light, upon the face of the matter or chaos; then he breathed light, into the face of man; and still he breaths and inspires light, into the face of his chosen. The poet, that beautified the sect, that was otherwise inferior to the rest, saith yet excellently well: It is a pleasure, to stand upon the shore, and to see ships tossed upon the sea; a pleasure, to stand in the window of a castle, and to see a battle, and the adventures thereof below: but no pleasure is comparable to the standing upon the vantage ground of truth (a hill not to be commanded, and where the air is always clear and serene), and to see the errors, and wanderings, and mists, and tempests, in the vale below; so always that this prospect be with pity, and not with swelling, or pride. Certainly, it is heaven upon earth, to have a man's mind move in charity, rest in providence, and turn upon the poles of truth.

To pass from theological, and philosophical truth, to the truth of civil business; it will be acknowledged, even by those that practise it not, that clear, and round dealing, is the honor of man's nature; and that mixture of falsehoods, is like alloy in coin of gold and silver, which may make the metal work the better, but it embases it. For these winding, and crooked courses, are the goings of the serpent; which goes basely upon the belly, and not upon the feet. There is no vice, that doth so cover a man with shame, as to be found false and perfidious. And therefore Montaigne saith prettily, when he inquired the reason, why the word of the lie should be such a disgrace, and such an odious charge? Saith he, If it be well weighed, to say that a man lies, is as much to say, as that he is brave towards God, and a coward towards men. For a lie faces God, and shrinks from man. Surely the wickedness of falsehood, and breach of faith, cannot possibly be so highly expressed, as in that it shall be the last peal, to call the judgments of God upon the generations of men; it being foretold, that when Christ comes, he shall not find faith upon the earth.

Moral 2: Of Unity

IN RELIGION

RELIGION being the chief band of human society, it is a happy thing, when itself is well contained within the true band of unity. The quarrels, and divisions about religion, were evils unknown to the heathen. The reason was, because the religion of the heathen, consisted rather in rites and ceremonies, than in any constant belief. For you may imagine, what kind of faith theirs was, when the chief doctors, and fathers of their church, were the poets. But the true God hath this attribute, that he is a jealous God; and therefore, his worship and religion, will endure no mixture, nor partner.We shall therefore speak a few words, concerning the unity of the church; what are the fruits thereof ; what the bounds; and what the means.

The fruits of unity (next unto the well pleasing of God, which is all in all) are two: the one, towards those that are without the church, the other, towards those that are within. For the former; it is certain, that heresies, and schisms, are of all others the greatest scandals; yea, more than corruption of manners. For as in the natural body, a wound, or solution of continuity, is worse than a corrupt humor; so in the spiritual. So that nothing, doth so much keep men out of the church, and drive men out of the church, as breach of unity. And therefore, whensoever it comes to that pass, that one saith, Ecce in deserto, another saith, Ecce in penetralibus; that is, when some men seek Christ, in the conventicles of heretics, and others, in an outward face of a church, that voice had need continually to sound in men's ears, Nolite exire, - Go not out. The doctor of the Gentiles (the propriety of whose vocation, drew him to have a special care of those without) saith, if an heathen come in, and hear you speak with several tongues, will he not say that you are mad? And certainly it is little better, when atheists, and profane persons, do hear of so many discordant, and contrary opinions in religion; it doth avert them from the church, and makes them, to sit down in the chair of the scorners. It is but a light thing, to be vouched in so serious a matter, but yet it expresses well the deformity. There is a master of scoffing, that in his catalogue of books of a feigned library, sets down this title of a book, The Morris-Dance of Heretics. For indeed, every sect of them, hath a diverse posture, or cringe by themselves, which cannot but move derision in worldlings, and depraved politics, who are apt to contemn holy things.

As for the fruit towards those that are within; it is peace; which contains infinite blessings. It establishes faith; it kindles charity; the outward peace of the church, distills into peace of conscience; and it turns the labors of writing, and reading of controversies, into treaties of mortification and devotion.

Concerning the bounds of unity; the true placing of them, imports exceedingly. There appear to be two extremes. For to certain zealants, all speech of pacification is odious. Is it peace, Jehu,? What hast thou to do with peace? turn thee behind me. Peace is not the matter, but following, and party. Contrariwise, certain Laodiceans, and lukewarm persons, think they may accommodate points of religion, by middle way, and taking part of both, and witty reconcilements; as if they would make an arbitrament between God and man. Both these extremes are to be avoided; which will be done, if the league of Christians, penned by our Savior himself, were in two cross clauses thereof, soundly and plainly expounded: He that is not with us, is against us; and again, He that is not against us, is with us; that is, if the points fundamental and of substance in religion, were truly discerned and distinguished, from points not merely of faith, but of opinion, order, or good intention. This is a thing may seem to many a matter trivial, and done already. But if it were done less partially, it would be embraced more generally.

Of this I may give only this advice, according to my small model. Men ought to take heed, of rending God's church, by two kinds of controversies. The one is, when the matter of the point controverted, is too small and light, not worth the heat and strife about it, kindled only by contradiction. For, as it is noted, by one of the fathers, Christ's coat indeed had no seam, but the church's vesture was of divers colors; whereupon he saith, In veste varietas sit, scissura non sit; they be two things, unity and uniformity. The other is, when the matter of the point controverted, is great, but it is driven to an over-great subtilty, and obscurity; so that it becomes a thing rather ingenious, than substantial. A man that is of judgment and understanding, shall sometimes hear ignorant men differ, and know well within himself, that those which so differ, mean one thing, and yet they themselves would never agree. And if it come so to pass, in that distance of judgment, which is between man and man, shall we not think that God above, that knows the heart, doth not discern that frail men, in some of their contradictions, intend the same thing; and accepts of both? The nature of such controversies is excellently expressed, by St. Paul, in the warning and precept, that he gives concerning the same, Devita profanas vocum novitates, et oppositiones falsi nominis scientiae. Men create oppositions, which are not; and put them into new terms, so fixed, as whereas the meaning ought to govern the term, the term in effect governs the meaning.There be also two false peaces, or unities: the one, when the peace is grounded, but upon an implicit ignorance; for all colors will agree in the dark: the other, when it is pieced up, upon a direct admission of contraries, in fundamental points. For truth and falsehood, in such things, are like the iron and clay, in the toes of Nebuchadnezzar's image; they may cleave, but they will not incorporate.

Concerning the means of procuring unity; men must beware, that in the procuring, or reuniting, of religious unity, they do not dissolve and deface the laws of charity, and of human society. There be two swords amongst Christians, the spiritual and temporal; and both have their due office and place, in the maintenance of religion. But we may not take up the third sword, which is Mahomet's sword, or like unto it; that is, to propagate religion by wars, or by sanguinary persecutions to force consciences; except it be in cases of overt scandal, blasphemy, or intermixture of practice against the state; much less to nourish seditions; to authorize conspiracies and rebellions; to put the sword into the people's hands;

and the like; tending to the subversion of all government, which is the ordinance of God. For this is but to dash the first table against the second; and so to consider men as Christians, as we forget that they are men. Lucretius the poet, when he beheld the act of Agamemnon, that could endure the sacrificing of his own daughter, exclaimed: Tantum Religio potuit suadere malorum.

What would he have said, if he had known of the massacre in France, or the powder treason of England? He would have been seven times more Epicure, and atheist, than he was. For as the temporal sword is to be drawn with great circumspection in cases of religion; so it is a thing monstrous to put it into the hands of the common people. Let that be left unto the Anabaptists, and other furies. It was great blasphemy, when the devil said, I will ascend, and be like the highest; but it is greater blasphemy, to personate God, and bring him in saying, I will descend, and be like the prince of darkness; and what is it better, to make the cause of religion to descend, to the cruel and execrable actions of murthering princes, butchery of people, and subversion of states and governments? Surely this is to bring down the Holy Ghost, instead of the likeness of a dove, in the shape of a vulture or raven; and set, out of the bark of a Christian church, a flag of a bark of pirates, and assassins. Therefore it is most necessary, that the church, by doctrine and decree, princes by their sword, and all learnings, both Christian and moral, as by their Mercury rod, do damn and send to hell for ever, those facts and opinions tending to the support of the same; as hath been already in good part done. Surely in counsels concerning religion, that counsel of the apostle would be prefixed, Ira hominis non implet justitiam Dei. And it was a notable observation of a wise father, and no less ingenuously confessed; that those which held and persuaded pressure of consciences, were commonly interested therein., themselves, for their own ends.

Moral 3: Of Revenge

REVENGE is a kind of wild justice; which the more man's nature runs to, the more ought law to weed it out. For as for the first wrong, it doth but offend the law; but the revenge of that wrong, putts the law out of office. Certainly, in taking revenge, a man is but even with his enemy; but in passing it over, he is superior; for it is a prince's part to pardon. And Solomon, I am sure, saith, It is the glory of a man, to pass by an offence. That which is past is gone, and irrevocable; and wise men have enough to do, with things present and to come; therefore they do but trifle with themselves, that labor in past matters. There is no man doth a wrong, for the wrong's sake; but thereby to purchase himself profit, or pleasure, or honor, or the like. Therefore why should I be angry with a man, for loving himself better than me? And if any man should do wrong, merely out of ill-nature, why, yet it is but like the thorn or briar, which prick and scratch, because they can do no other. The most tolerable sort of revenge, is for those wrongs which there is no law to remedy; but then let a man take heed, the revenge be such as there is no law to punish; else a man's enemy is still before hand, and it is two for one. Some, when they take revenge, are desirous, the party should know, whence it comes. This is the more generous. For the delight seems to be, not so much in doing the hurt, as in making the party repent. But base and crafty cowards, are like the arrow that flies in the dark. Cosmus, duke of Florence, had a desperate saying against perfidious or neglecting friends, as if those wrongs were unpardonable; You shall read (saith he) that we are commanded to forgive our enemies; but you never read, that we are commanded to forgive our friends. But yet the spirit of Job was in a better tune: Shall we (saith he) take good at God's hands, and not be content to take evil also? And so of friends in a proportion. This is certain, that a man that studies revenge, keeps his own wounds green, which otherwise would heal, and do well. Public revenges are for the most part fortunate; as that for the death of Caesar; for the death of Pertinax; for the death of Henry the Third of France; and many more. But in private revenges, it is not so. Nay rather, vindictive persons live the life of witches; who, as they are mischievous, so end they infortunate.

Moral 4: Of Adversity

IT WAS an high speech of Seneca (after the manner of the Stoics), that the good things, which belong to prosperity, are to be wished; but the good things, that belong to adversity, are to be admired. Bona rerum secundarum optabilia; adversarum mirabilia. Certainly if miracles be the command over nature, they appear most in adversity. It is yet a higher speech of his, than the other (much too high for a heathen), It is true greatness, to have in one the frailty of a man, and the security of a God. Vere magnum habere fragilitatem hominis, securitatem Dei. This would have done better in poesy, where transcendences are more allowed. And the poets indeed have been busy with it; for it is in effect the thing, which figured in that strange fiction of the ancient poets, which seems not to be without mystery; nay, and to have some approach to the state of a Christian; that Hercules, when he went to unbind Prometheus (by whom human nature is represented), sailed the length of the great ocean, in an earthen pot or pitcher; lively describing Christian resolution, that sails in the frail bark of the flesh, through the waves of the world. But to speak in a mean. The virtue of prosperity, is temperance; the virtue of adversity, is fortitude; which in morals is the more heroical virtue. Prosperity is the blessing of the Old Testament; adversity is the blessing of the New; which carries the greater benediction, and the clearer revelation of God's favor. Yet even in the Old Testament, if you listen to David's harp, you shall hear as many hearse-like airs as carols; and the pencil of the Holy Ghost hath labored more in describing the afflictions of Job, than the felicities of Solomon. Prosperity is not without many fears and distastes; and adversity is not without comforts and hopes. We see in needle-works and embroideries, it is more pleasing to have a lively work, upon a sad and solemn ground, than to have a dark and melancholy work, upon a lightsome ground: judge therefore of the pleasure of the heart, by the pleasure of the eye. Certainly virtue is like precious odors, most fragrant when they are incensed, or crushed: for prosperity doth best discover vice, but adversity doth best discover virtue.

Moral 5: Of Envy

THERE be none of the affections, which have been noted to fascinate or bewitch, but love and envy. They both have vehement wishes; they frame themselves readily into imaginations and suggestions; and they come easily into the eye, especially upon the present of the objects; which are the points that conduce to fascination, if any such thing there be. We see likewise, the Scripture calls envy an evil eye; and the astrologers, call the evil influences of the stars, evil aspects; so that still there seems to be acknowledged, in the act of envy, an ejaculation or irradiation of the eye. Nay, some have been so curious, as to note, that the times when the stroke or percussion of an envious eye doth most hurt, are when the party envied is beheld in glory or triumph; for that sets an edge upon envy: and besides, at such times the spirits of the person envied, do come forth most into the outward parts, and so meet the blow.

But leaving these curiosities (though not unworthy to be thought on, in fit place), we will handle, what persons are apt to envy others; what persons are most subject to be envied themselves; and what is the difference between public and private envy.

A man that hath no virtue in himself, ever envies virtue in others. For men's minds, will either feed upon their own good, or upon others' evil; and who wants the one, will prey upon the other; and whoso is out of hope, to attain to another's virtue, will seek to come at even hand, by depressing another's fortune.

A man that is busy, and inquisitive, is commonly envious. For to know much of other men's matters, cannot be because all that ado may concern his own estate; therefore it must needs be, that he takes a kind of play-pleasure, in looking upon the fortunes of others. Neither can he, that minds but his own business, find much matter for envy. For envy is a gadding passion, and walks the streets, and doth not keep home: Non est curiosus, quin idem sit malevolus.

Men of noble birth, are noted to be envious towards new men, when they rise. For the distance is altered, and it is like a deceit of the eye, that when others come on, they think themselves, go back.

Deformed persons, and eunuchs, and old men, and bastards, are envious. For he that cannot possibly mend his own case, will do what he can, to impair another's; except these defects light upon a very brave, and heroical nature, which thinks to make his natural wants part of his honor; in that it should be said, that an eunuch, or a lame man, did such great matters; affecting the honor of a miracle; as it was in Narses the eunuch, and Agesilaus and Tamberlanes, that were lame men.

The same is the case of men, that rise after calamities and misfortunes. For they are as men fallen out with the times; and think other men's harms, a redemption of their own sufferings.

They that desire to excel in too many matters, out of levity and vain glory, are ever envious. For they cannot want work; it being impossible, but many, in some one of those things, should surpass them. Which was the character of Adrian the Emperor; that mortally envied poets, and painters, and artificers, in works wherein he had a vein to excel.

Lastly, near kinsfolks, and fellows in office, and those that have been bred together, are more apt to envy their equals, when they are raised. For it doth upbraid unto them their own fortunes, and points at them, and comes oftener into their remembrance, and incurrs likewise more into the note of others; and envy ever redoubles from speech and fame. Cain's envy was the more vile and malignant, towards his brother Abel, because when his sacrifice was better accepted, there was no body to look on. Thus much for those, that are apt to envy.

Concerning those that are more or less subject to envy: First, persons of eminent virtue, when they are advanced, are less envied. For their fortune seems , but due unto them; and no man envies the payment of a debt, but rewards and liberality rather. Again, envy is ever joined with the comparing of a man's self; and where there is no comparison, no envy; and therefore kings are not envied, but by kings. Nevertheless it is to be noted, that unworthy persons are most envied, at their first coming in, and afterwards overcome it better; whereas contrariwise, persons of worth and merit are most envied, when their fortune continues long. For by that time, though their virtue be the same, yet it hath not the same lustre; for fresh men grow up that darken it.

Persons of noble blood, are less envied in their rising. For it seems but right done to their birth. Besides, there seems not much added to their fortune; and envy is as the sunbeams, that beat hotter upon a bank, or steep rising ground, than upon a flat. And for the same reason, those that are advanced by degrees, are less envied than those that are advanced suddenly and per saltum.

Those that have joined with their honor great travels, cares, or perils, are less subject to envy. For men think that they earn their honors hardly, and pity them sometimes; and pity ever heals envy. Wherefore you shall observe, that the more deep and sober sort of politic persons, in their greataess, are ever bemoaning themselves, what a life they lead; chanting a quanta patimur! Not that they feel it so, but only to abate the edge of envy. But this is to be understood, of business that is laid upon men, and not such, as they call unto themselves. For nothing increases envy more, than an unnecessary and ambitious engrossing of business. And nothing doth extinguish envy more, than for a great person to preserve all other inferior officers, in their full lights and pre-eminences of their places. For by that means, there be so many screens between him and envy.

Above all, those are most subject to envy, which carry the greatness of their fortunes, in an insolent and proud manner; being never well, but while they are showing how great they are, either by outward pomp, or by triumphing over all opposition or competition; whereas wise men will rather do sacrifice to envy, in suffering themselves sometimes of purpose to be crossed, and overborne in things that do not much concern them. Notwithstanding, so much is true, that the carriage of greatness, in a plain and open manner (so it be without arrogancy and vain glory) doth draw less envy, than if it be in a more crafty and cunning fashion. For in that course, a man doth but disavow fortune; and seems to be conscious of his own want in worth; and doth but teach others, to envy him.

Lastly, to conclude this part; as we said in the beginning, that the act of envy had somewhat in it of witchcraft, so there is no other cure of envy, but the cure of witchcraft; and that is, to remove the lot (as they call it) and to lay it upon another. For which purpose, the wiser sort of great persons, bring in ever upon the stage somebody upon whom to derive the envy, that would come upon themselves; sometimes upon ministers and servants; sometimes upon colleagues and associates; and the like; and for that turn there are never wanting, some persons of violent and undertaking natures, who, so they may have power and business, will take it at any cost.

Now, to speak of public envy. There is yet some good in public envy, whereas in private, there is none. For public envy, is as an ostracism, that eclipses men, when they grow too great. And therefore it is a bridle also to great ones, to keep them within bounds.

This envy, being in the Latin word invidia, goes in the modern language, by the name of discontentment; of which we shall speak, in handling sedition. It is a disease, in a state, like to infection. For as infection spreads upon that which is sound, and taints it; so when envy is gotten once into a state, it traduces even the best actions thereof, and turns them into an ill odor. And therefore there is little won, by intermingling of plausible actions. For that doth argue but a weakness, and fear of envy, which hurts so much the more, as it is likewise usual in infections; which if you fear them, you call them upon you.

This public envy, seems to beat chiefly upon principal officers or ministers, rather than upon kings, and estates themselves. But this is a sure rule, that if the envy upon the minister be great, when the cause of it in him is small; or if the envy be general, in a manner upon all the ministers of an estate; then the envy (though hidden) is truly upon the state itself. And so much of public envy or discontentment, and the difference thereof from private envy, which was handled in the first place.

We will add this in general, touching the affection of envy; that of all other affections, it is the most importune and continual. For of other affections, there is occasion given, but now and then; and therefore it was well said, Invidia festos dies non agit: for it is ever working upon some or other. And it is also noted, that love and envy do make a man pine, which other affections do not, because they are not so continual. It is also the vilest affection, and the most depraved; for which cause it is the proper attribute of the devil, who is called, the envious man, that sows tares amongst the wheat by night; as it always comes to pass, that envy works subtilly, and in the dark, and to the prejudice of good things, such as is the wheat.

Moral 6: Of Love

THE stage is more beholding to love, than the life of man. For as to the stage, love is ever matter of comedies, and now and then of tragedies; but in life it doth much mischief; sometimes like a siren, sometimes like a fury. You may observe, that amongst all the great and worthy persons (whereof the memory remains, either ancient or recent) there is not one, that hath been transported to the mad degree of love: which shows that great spirits, and great business, do keep out this weak passion. You must except, nevertheless, Marcus Antonius, the half partner of the empire of Rome, and Appius Claudius, the decemvir and lawgiver; whereof the former was indeed a voluptuous man, and inordinate; but the latter was an austere and wise man: and therefore it seems (though rarely) that love can find entrance, not only into an open heart, but also into a heart well fortified, if watch be not well kept. It is a poor saying of Epicurus, Satis magnum alter alteri theatrum sumus; as if man, made for the contemplation of heaven, and all noble objects, should do nothing but kneel before a little idol, and make himself a subject, though not of the mouth (as beasts are), yet of the eye; which was given him for higher purposes. It is a strange thing, to note the excess of this passion, and how it braves the nature, and value of things, by this; that the speaking in a perpetual hyperbole, is comely in nothing but in love. Neither is it merely in the phrase; for whereas it hath been well said, that the arch-flatterer, with whom all the petty flatterers have intelligence, is a man's self; certainly the lover is more. For there was never proud man thought so absurdly well of himself, as the lover doth of the person loved; and therefore it was well said, That it is impossible to love, and to be wise. Neither doth this weakness appear to others only, and not to the party loved; but to the loved most of all, except the love be reciproque. For it is a true rule, that love is ever rewarded, either with the reciproque, or with an inward and secret contempt. By how much the more, men ought to beware of this passion, which loses not only other things, but itself! As for the other losses, the poet's relation doth well figure them: that he that preferred Helena, quitted the gifts of Juno and Pallas. For whosoever esteems too much of amorous affection, quits both riches and wisdom. This passion hath his floods, in very times of weakness; which are great prosperity, and great adversity; though this latter hath been less observed: both which times kindle love, and make it more fervent, and therefore show it to be the child of folly. They do best, who if they cannot but admit love, yet make it keep quarters; and sever it wholly from their serious affairs, and actions, of life; for if it check once with business, it troubles men's fortunes, and makes men, that they can no ways be true to their own ends. I know not how, but martial men are given to love: I think, it is but as they are given to wine; for perils commonly ask to be paid in pleasures. There is in man's nature, a secret inclination and motion, towards love of others, which if it be not spent upon some one or a few, doth naturally spread itself towards many, and makes men become humane and charitable; as it is seen sometime in friars. Nuptial love makes mankind; friendly love perfects it; but wanton love corrupts, and embases it.

Moral 7: Of Anger

TO SEEK to extinguish anger utterly, is but a bravery of the Stoics. We have better oracles: Be angry, but sin not. Let not the sun go down upon your anger. Anger must be limited and confined, both in race and in time. We will first speak how the natural inclination and habit to be angry, may be attempted and calmed. Secondly, how the particular motions of anger may be repressed, or at least refrained from doing mischief. Thirdly, how to raise anger, or appease anger in another.

For the first; there is no other way but to meditate, and ruminate well upon the effects of anger, how it troubles man's life. And the best time to do this, is to look back upon anger, when the fit is thoroughly over. Seneca saith well, That anger is like ruin, which breaks itself upon that it falls. The Scripture exhorts us to possess our souls in patience. Whosoever is out of patience, is out of possession of his soul. Men must not turn bees;

... animasque in vulnere ponunt.

Anger is certainly a kind of baseness; as it appears well in the weakness of those subjects in whom it reigns; children, women, old folks, sick folks. Only men must beware, that they carry their anger rather with scorn, than with fear; so that they may seem rather to be above the injury, than below it; which is a thing easily done, if a man will give law to himself in it.

For the second point; the causes and motives of anger, are chiefly three. First, to be too sensible of hurt; for no man is angry, that feels not himself hurt; and therefore tender and delicate persons must needs be oft angry; they have so many things to trouble them, which more robust natures have little sense of. The next is, the apprehension and construction of the injury offered, to be, in the circumstances thereof, full of contempt: for contempt is that, which putts an edge upon anger, as much or more than the hurt itself. And therefore, when men are ingenious in picking out circumstances of contempt, they do kindle their anger much. Lastly, opinion of the touch of a man's reputation, doth multiply and sharpen anger. Wherein the remedy is, that a man should have, as Consalvo was wont to say, telam honoris crassiorem. But in all refrainings of anger, it is the best remedy to win time; and to make a man's self believe, that the opportunity of his revenge is not yet come, but that he foresees a time for it; and so to still himself in the meantime, and reserve it.

To contain anger from mischief, though it take hold of a man, there be two things, whereof you must have special caution. The one, of extreme bitterness of words, especially if they be aculeate and proper; for cummunia maledicta are nothing so much; and again, that in anger a man reveal no secrets; for that, makes him not fit for society. The other, that you do not peremptorily break off, in any business, in a fit of anger; but howsoever you show bitterness, do not act anything, that is not revocable.

For raising and appeasing anger in another; it is done chiefly by choosing of times, when men are frowardest and worst disposed, to incense them. Again, by gathering (as was touched before) all that you can find out, to aggravate the contempt. And the two remedies are by the contraries. The former to take good times, when first to relate to a man an angry business; for the first impression is much; and the other is, to sever, as much as may be, the construction of the injury from the point of contempt; imputing it to misunderstanding, fear, passion, or what you will.

Moral 8: Of Fame

THE poets make Fame a monster. They describe her in part finely and elegantly, and in part gravely and sententiously. They say, look how many feathers she hath, so many eyes she hath underneath; so many tongues; so many voices; she pricks up so many ears.

This is a flourish. There follow excellent parables; as that, she gathers strength in going; that she goes upon the ground, and yet hides her head in the clouds; that in the daytime she sits in a watch tower, and flies most by night; that she mingles things done, with things not done; and that she is a terror to great cities. But that which passes all the rest is: They do recount that the Earth, mother of the giants that made war against Jupiter, and were by him destroyed, thereupon in an anger brought forth Fame. For certain it is, that rebels, figured by the giants, and seditious fames and libels, are but brothers and sisters, masculine and feminine. But now, if a man can tame this monster, and bring her to feed at the hand, and govern her, and with her fly other ravening fowl and kill them, it is somewhat worth. But we are infected with the style of the poets. To speak now in a sad and serious manner: There is not, in all the politics, a place less handled and more worthy to be handled, than this of fame. We will therefore speak of these points: What are false fames; and what are true fames; and how they may be best discerned; how fames may be sown, and raised; how they may be spread, and multiplied; and how they may be checked, and laid dead. And other things concerning the nature of fame. Fame is of that force, as there is scarcely any great action, wherein it hath not a great part; especially in the war. Mucianus undid Vitellius, by a fame that he scattered, that Vitellius had in purpose to remove the legions of Syria into Germany, and the legions of Germany into Syria; whereupon the legions of Syria were infinitely inflamed. Julius Caesar took Pompey unprovided, and laid asleep his industry and preparations, by a fame that he cunningly gave out: Caesar's own soldiers loved him not, and being wearied with the wars, and laden with the spoils of Gaul, would forsake him, as soon as he came into Italy. Livia settled all things for the succession of her son Tiberius, by continual giving out, that her husband Augustus was upon recovery and amendment, and it is an usual thing with the pashas, to conceal the death of the Great Turk from the janizaries and men of war, to save the sacking of Constantinople and other towns, as their manner is. Themistocles made Xerxes, king of Persia, post apace out of Grecia, by giving out, that the Grecians had a purpose to break his bridge of ships, which he had made athwart Hellespont. There be a thousand such like examples; and the more they are, the less they need to be repeated; because a man meets with them everywhere. Therefore let all wise governors have as great a watch and care over fames, as they have of the actions and designs themselves.

Moral 9: Of Praise

PRAISE is the reflection of virtue; but it is as the glass or body, which gives the reflection. If it be from the common people, it is commonly false and naught; and rather follows vain persons, than virtuous. For the common people understand not many excellent virtues. The lowest virtues draw praise from them; the middle virtues work in them astonishment or admiration; but of the highest virtues, they have no sense of perceiving at all. But shows, and species virtutibus similes, serve best with them. Certainly fame is like a river, that bears up things light and swoln, and drowns things weighty and solid. But if persons of quality and judgment concur, then it is (as the Scripture saith) nomen bonum instar unguenti fragrantis. It fires all round about, and will not easily away. For the odors of ointments are more durable, than those of flowers. There be so many false points of praise, that a man may justly hold it a suspect. Some praises proceed merely of flattery; and if he be an ordinary flatterer, he will have certain common attributes, which may serve every man; if he be a cunning flatterer, he will follow the archflatterer, which is a man's self; and wherein a man thinks best of himself, therein the flatterer will uphold him most: but if he be an impudent flatterer, look wherein a man is conscious to himself, that he is most defective, and is most out of countenance in himself, that will the flatterer entitle him to perforce, spreta conscientia. Some praises come of good wishes and respects, which is a form due, in civility, to kings and great persons, laudando praecipere, when by telling men what they are, they represent to them, what they should be. Some men are praised maliciously, to their hurt, thereby to stir envy and jealousy towards them: pessimum genus inimicorum laudantium; insomuch as it was a proverb, amongst the Grecians, that he that was praised to his hurt, should have a push rise upon his nose; as we say, that a blister will rise upon one's tongue, that tells a lie. Certainly moderate praise, used with opportunity, and not vulgar, is that which doth the good. Solomon saith, He that praises his friend aloud, rising early, it shall be to him no better than a curse. Too much magnifying of man or matter, doth irritate contradiction, and procure envy and scorn. To praise a man's self, cannot be decent, except it be in rare cases; but to praise a man's office or profession, he may do it with good grace, and with a kind of magnanimity. The cardinals of Rome, which are theologues, and friars, and Schoolmen, have a phrase of notable contempt and scorn towards civil business: for they call all temporal business of wars, embassages, judicature, and other employments, sbirrerie, which is under-sheriffries; as if they were but matters, for under-sheriffs and catchpoles: though many times those under-sheriffries do more good, than their high speculations. St. Paul, when he boasts of himself, he doth oft interlace, I speak like a fool; but speaking of his calling, he saith, magnificabo apostolatum meum.

Moral 10: Of Wisdom

AN ANT is a wise creature for itself, but it is a shrewd thing, in an orchard or garden. And certainly, men that are great lovers of themselves, waste the public. Divide with reason; between selflove and society; and be so true to thyself, as thou be not false to others; specially to thy king and country. It is a poor centre of a man's actions, himself. It is right earth. For that only stands fast upon his own centre; whereas all things, that have affinity with the heavens, move upon the centre of another, which they benefit. The referring of all to a man's self, is more tolerable in a sovereign prince; because themselves are not only themselves, but their good and evil is at the peril of the public fortune. But it is a desperate evil, in a servant to a prince, or a citizen in a republic. For whatsoever affairs pass such a man's hands, he crooks them to his own ends; which must needs be often eccentric to the ends of his master, or state. Therefore, let princes, or states, choose such servants, as have not this mark; except they mean their service should be made but the accessory. That which maks the effect more pernicious, is that all proportion is lost. It were disproportion enough, for the servant's good to be preferred before the master's; but yet it is a greater extreme, when a little good of the servant, shall carry things against a great good of the master's. And yet that is the case of bad officers, treasurers, ambassadors, generals, and other false and corrupt servants; which set a bias upon their bowl, of their own petty ends and envies, to the overthrow of their master's great and important affairs. And for the most part, the good such servants receive, is after the model of their own fortune; but the hurt they sell for that good, is after the model of their master's fortune. And certainly it is the nature of extreme self-lovers, as they will set an house on fire, and it were but to roast their eggs; and yet these men many times hold credit with their masters, because their study is but to please them, and profit themselves; and for either respect, they will abandon the good of their affairs.

Wisdom for a man's self is, in many branches thereof, a depraved thing. It is the wisdom of rats, that will be sure to leave a house, somewhat before it fall. It is the wisdom of the fox, that thrusts out the badger, who digged and made room for him. It is the wisdom of crocodiles, that shed tears when they would devour. But that which is specially to be noted is, that those which (as Cicero says of Pompey) are sui amantes, sine rivali, are many times unfortunate. And whereas they have, all their times, sacrificed to themselves, they become in the end, themselves sacrifices to the inconstancy of fortune, whose wings they thought, by their self-wisdom, to have pinioned.

Moral 11: Of Troubles

AND SEDITIONS

SHEPHERDS of people, had need know the calendars of tempests in state; which are commonly greatest, when things grow to equality; as natural tempests are greatest about the Equinoctia. And as there are certain hollow blasts of wind, and secret swellings of seas before a tempest, so are there in states:

--Ille etiam caecos instare tumultus Saepe monet, fraudesque et operta tunescere bella.

Libels and licentious discourses against the state, when they are frequent and open; and in like sort, false news often running up and down, to the disadvantage of the state, and hastily embraced; are amongst the signs of troubles. Virgil, giving the pedigree of Fame, saith, she was sister to the Giants:

Illam Terra parens, irra irritata deorum, Extremam (ut perhibent) Coeo Enceladoque sororem Progenuit.-

As if fames were the relics of seditions past; but they are no less, indeed, the preludes of seditions to come. Howsoever he notes it right, that seditious tumults, and seditious fames, differ no more but as brother and sister, masculine and feminine; especially if it come to that, that the best actions of a state, and the most plausible, and which ought to give greatest contentment, are taken in ill sense, and traduced: for that shows the envy great, as Tacitus saith; conflata magna invidia, seu bene seu male gesta premunt. Neither doth it follow, that because these fames are a sign of troubles, that the suppressing of them with too much severity, should be a remedy of troubles. For the despising of them, many times checks them best; and the going about to stop them, doth but make a wonder long-lived. Also that kind of obedience, which Tacitus speaks of, is to be held suspected: Erant in officio, sed tamen qui mallent mandata imperantium interpretari quam exequi; disputing, excusing, cavilling upon mandates and directions, is a kind of shaking off the yoke, and assay of disobedience; especially if in those disputings, they which are for the direction, speak fearfully and tenderly, and those that are against it, audaciously.

Also, as Machiavel notes well, when princes, that ought to be common parents, make themselves as a party, and lean to a side, it is as a boat, that is overthrown by uneven weight on the one side; as was well seen, in the time of Henry the Third of France; for first, himself entered league for the extirpation of the Protestants; and presently after, the same league was turned upon himself. For when the authority of princes, is made but an accessory to a cause, and that there be other bands, that tie faster than the band of sovereignty, kings begin to be put almost out of possession.

Also, when discords, and quarrels, and factions are carried openly and audaciously, it is a sign the reverence of government is lost. For the motions of the greatest persons in a government, ought to be as the motions of the planets under primum mobile; according to the old opinion: which is, that every of them, is carried swiftly by the highest motion, and softly in their own motion. And therefore, when great ones in their own particular motion, move violently, and, as Tacitus expresses it well, liberius quam ut imperantium meminissent; it is a sign the orbs are out of frame. For reverence is that, wherewith princes are girt from God; who threatens the dissolving thereof; Solvam cingula regum.

So when any of the four pillars of government, are mainly shaken, or weakened (which are religion, justice, counsel, and treasure), men had need to pray for fair weather. But let us pass from this part of predictions (concerning which, nevertheless, more light may be taken from that which follows); and let us speak first, of the materials of seditions; then of the motives of them; and thirdly of the remedies.

Concerning the materials of seditions. It is a thing well to be considered; for the surest way to prevent seditions (if the times do bear it) is to take away the matter of them. For if there be fuel prepared, it is hard to tell, whence the spark shall come, that shall set it on fire. The matter of seditions is of two kinds: much poverty, and much discontentment. It is certain, so many overthrown estates, so many votes for troubles. Lucan notes well the state of Rome before the Civil War,

Hinc usura vorax, rapidumque in tempore foenus, Hinc concussa fides, et multis utile bellum.

This same multis utile bellum, is an assured and infallible sign, of a state disposed to seditions and troubles. And if this poverty and broken estate in the better sort, be joined with a want and necessity in the mean people, the danger is imminent and great. For the rebellions of the belly are the worst. As for discontentments, they are, in the politic body, like to humors in the natural, which are apt to gather a preternatural heat, and to inflame. And let no prince measure the danger of them by this, whether they be just or unjust: for that were to imagine people, to be too reasonable; who do often spurn at their own good: nor yet by this, whether the griefs whereupon they rise, be in fact great or small: for they are the most dangerous discontentments, where the fear is greater than the feeling. Dolendi modus, timendi non item. Besides, in great oppressions, the same things that provoke the patience, do withal mate the courage; but in fears it is not so. Neither let any prince, or state, be secure concerning discontentments, because they have been often, or have been long, and yet no peril hath ensued: for as it is true, that every vapor or fume doth not turn into a storm; so it is nevertheless true, that storms, though they blow over divers times, yet may fall at last; and, as the Spanish proverb notes well, The cord breaks at the last by the weakest pull.

The causes and motives of seditions are, innovation in religion; taxes; alteration of laws and customs; breaking of privileges; general oppression; advancement of unworthy persons; strangers; dearths;

disbanded soldiers; factions grown desperate; and what soever, in offending people, joins and knits them in a common cause.

For the remedies; there may be some general preservatives, whereof we will speak: as for the just cure, it must answer to the particular disease; and so be left to counsel, rather than rule.

The first remedy or prevention is to remove, by all means possible, that material cause of sedition whereof we spake; which is, want and poverty in the estate. To which purpose serves the opening, and well-balancing of trade; the cherishing of manufactures; the banishing of idleness; the repressing of waste, and excess, by sumptuary laws; the improvement and husbanding of the soil; the regulating of prices of things vendible; the moderating of taxes and tributes; and the like. Generally, it is to be foreseen that the population of a kingdom (especially if it be not mown down by wars) do not exceed the stock of the kingdom, which should maintain them. Neither is the population to be reckoned only by number; for a smaller number, that spend more and earn less, do wear out an estate sooner, than a greater number that live lower, and gather more. Therefore the multiplying of nobility, and other degrees of quality, in an over proportion to the common people, doth speedily bring a state to necessity; and so doth likewise an overgrown clergy; for they bring nothing to the stock; and in like manner, when more are bred scholars, than preferments can take off .

It is likewise to be remembered, that forasmuch as the increase of any estate must be upon the foreigner (for whatsoever is somewhere gotten, is somewhere lost), there be but three things, which one nation sells unto another; the commodity as nature yields it; the manufacture; and the vecture, or carriage. So that if these three wheels go, wealth will flow as in a spring tide. And it comes many times to pass, that materiam superabit opus; that the work and carriage is more worth than the material, and enrichs a state more; as is notably seen in the Low-Countrymen, who have the best mines above ground, in the world.

Above all things, good policy is to be used, that the treasure and moneys, in a state, be not gathered into few hands. For otherwise a state may have a great stock, and yet starve. And money is like muck, not good except it be spread. This is done, chiefly by suppressing, or at least keeping a strait hand, upon the devouring trades of usury, ingrossing great pasturages, and the like.

For removing discontentments, or at least the danger of them; there is in every state (as we know) two portions of subjects; the noblesse and the commonalty. When one of these is discontent, the danger is not great; for common people are of slow motion, if they be not excited by the greater sort; and the greater sort are of small strength, except the multitude be apt, and ready to move of themselves. Then is the danger, when the greater sort, do but wait for the troubling of the waters amongst the meaner, that then they may declare themselves. The poets feign, that the rest of the gods would have bound Jupiter; which he hearing of, by the counsel of Pallas, sent for Briareus, with his hundred hands, to come in to his aid. An emblem, no doubt, to show how safe it is for monarchs, to make sure of the good will of common people. To give moderate liberty for griefs and discontentments to evaporate (so it be without too great insolency or bravery), is a safe way. For he that turns the humors back, and makes the wound bleed inwards, endangers malign ulcers, and pernicious imposthumations.

The part of Epimetheus mought well become Prometheus, in the case of discontentments: for there is not a better provision against them. Epimetheus, when griefs and evils flew abroad, at last shut the lid, and kept hope in the bottom of the vessel. Certainly, the politic and artificial nourishing, and entertaining of hopes, and carrying men from hopes to hopes, is one of the best antidotes against the poison of discontentments. And it is a certain sign of a wise government and proceeding, when it can hold men's hearts by hopes, when it cannot by satisfaction; and when it can handle things, in such manner, as no evil shall appear so peremptory, but that it hath some outlet of hope; which is the less hard to do, because both particular persons and factions, are apt enough to flatter themselves, or at least to brave that, which they believe not.

Also the foresight and prevention, that there be no likely or fit head, whereunto discontented persons may resort, and under whom they may join, is a known, but an excellent point of caution. I understand a fit head, to be one that hath greatness and reputation; that hath confidence with the discontented party, and upon whom they turn their eyes; and that is thought discontented, in his own particular: which kind of persons, are either to be won, and reconciled to the state, and that in a fast and true manner; or to be fronted with some other, of the same party, that may oppose them, and so divide the reputation. Generally, the dividing and breaking, of all factions and combinations that are adverse to the state, and setting them at distance, or at least distrust, amongst themselves, is not one of the worst remedies. For it is a desperate case, if those that hold with the proceeding of the state, be full of discord and faction, and those that are against it, be entire and united.

I have noted, that some witty and sharp speeches, which have fallen from princes, have given fire to seditions. Caesar did himself infinite hurt in that speech, Sylla nescivit literas, non potuit dictare; for it did utterly cut off that hope, which men had entertained, that he would at one time or other give over his dictatorship. Galba undid himself by that speech, legi a se militem, non emi; for it put the soldiers out of hope of the donative. Probus likewise, by that speech, Si vixero, non opus erit amplius Romano imperio militibus; a speech of great despair for the soldiers. And many the like. Surely princes had need, in tender matters and ticklish times, to beware what they say; especially in these short speeches, which fly abroad like darts, and are thought to be shot out of their secret intentions. For as for large discourses, they are flat things, and not so much noted.

Lastly, let princes, against all events, not be without some great person, one or rather more, of military valor, near unto them, for the repressing of seditions in their beginnings. For without that, there uses to be more trepidation in court upon the first breaking out of troubles, than were fit. And the state runs the danger of that which Tacitus saith; Atque is habitus animorum fuit, ut pessimum facinus auderent pauci, plures vellent, omnes paterentur. But let such military persons be assured, and well reputed of, rather than factious and popular; holding also good correspondence with the other great men in the state; or else the remedy, is worse than the disease.

Moral 12: Of Friendship

IT HAD been hard for him that spake it to have put more truth and untruth together in few words, than in that speech, Whatsoever is delighted in solitude, is either a wild beast or a god. For it is most true, that a natural and secret hatred, and aversation towards society, in any man, hath somewhat of the savage beast; but it is most untrue, that it should have any character at all, of the divine nature; except it proceed, not out of a pleasure in solitude, but out of a love and desire to sequester a man's self, for a higher conversation: such as is found to have been falsely and feignedly in some of the heathen; as Epimenides the Candian, Numa the Roman, Empedocles the Sicilian, and Apollonius of Tyana; and truly and really, in divers of the ancient hermits and holy fathers of the church. But little do men perceive what solitude is, and how far it extends. For a crowd is not company; and faces are but a gallery of pictures; and talk but a tinkling cymbal, where there is no love. The Latin adage meets with it a little: Magna civitas, magna solitudo; because in a great town friends are scattered; so that there is not that fellowship, for the most part, which is in less neighborhoods. But we may go further, and affirm most truly, that it is a mere and miserable solitude to want true friends; without which the world is but a wilderness; and even in this sense also of solitude, whosoever in the frame of his nature and affections, is unfit for friendship, he takes it of the beast, and not from humanity.

A principal fruit of friendship, is the ease and discharge of the fulness and swellings of the heart, which passions of all kinds do cause and induce. We know diseases of stoppings, and suffocations, are the most dangerous in the body; and it is not much otherwise in the mind; you may take sarza to open the liver, steel to open the spleen, flowers of sulphur for the lungs, castoreum for the brain; but no receipt opens the heart, but a true friend; to whom you may impart griefs, joys, fears, hopes, suspicions, counsels, and whatsoever lies upon the heart to oppress it, in a kind of civil shrift or confession.

It is a strange thing to observe, how high a rate great kings and monarchs do set upon this fruit of friendship, whereof we speak: so great, as they purchase it, many times, at the hazard of their own safety and greatness. For princes, in regard of the distance of their fortune from that of their subjects and servants, cannot gather this fruit, except (to make themselves capable thereof) they raise some persons to be, as it were, companions and almost equals to themselves, which many times sorts to inconvenience. The modern languages give unto such persons the name of favorites, or privadoes; as if it were matter of grace, or conversation. But the Roman name attains the true use and cause thereof, naming them participes curarum; for it is that which ties the knot. And we see plainly that this hath been done, not by weak and passionate princes only, but by the wisest and most politic that ever reigned; who have oftentimes joined to themselves some of their servants; whom both themselves have called friends, and allowed other likewise to call them in the same manner; using the word which is received between private men.

L. Sylla, when he commanded Rome, raised Pompey (after surnamed the Great) to that height, that Pompey vaunted himself for Sylla's overmatch. For when he had carried the consulship for a friend of his, against the pursuit of Sylla, and that Sylla did a little resent thereat, and began to speak great, Pompey turned upon him again, and in effect bade him be quiet; for that more men adored the sun rising, than the sun setting. With Julius Caesar, Decimus Brutus had obtained that interest as he set him down in his testament, for heir in remainder, after his nephew. And this was the man that had power with him, to draw him forth to his death. For when Caesar would have discharged the senate, in regard of some ill presages, and specially a dream of Calpurnia; this man lifted him gently by the arm out of his chair, telling him he hoped he would not dismiss the senate, till his wife had dreamt a better dream. And it seems his favor was so great, as Antonius, in a letter which is recited verbatim in one of Cicero's Philippics, calls him venefica, witch; as if he had enchanted Caesar. Augustus raised Agrippa (though of mean birth) to that height, as when he consulted with Maecenas, about the marriage of his daughter Julia, Maecenas took the liberty to tell him, that he must either marry his daughter to Agrippa, or take away his life; there was no third way, he had made him so great. With Tiberius Caesar, Sejanus had ascended to that height, as they two were termed, and reckoned, as a pair of friends. Tiberius in a letter to him saith, Haec pro amicitia nostra non occultavi; and the whole senate dedicated an altar to Friendship, as to a goddess, in respect of the great dearness of friendship, between them two. The like, or more, was between Septimius Severus and Plautianus. For he forced his eldest son to marry the daughter of Plautianus; and would often maintain Plautianus, in doing affronts to his son; and did write also in a letter to the senate, by these words: I love the man so well, as I wish he may over-live me. Now if these princes had been as a Trajan, or a Marcus Aurelius, a man might have thought that this had proceeded of an abundant goodness of nature; but being men so wise, of such strength and severity of mind, and so extreme lovers of themselves, as all these were, it proves most plainly that they found their own felicity (though as great as ever happened to mortal men) but as an half piece, except they mought have a friend, to make it entire; and yet, which is more, they were princes that had wives, sons, nephews; and yet all these could not supply the comfort of friendship.

It is not to be forgotten, what Comineus observes of his first master, Duke Charles the Hardy, namely, that he would communicate his secrets with none; and least of all, those secrets which troubled him most. Whereupon he goes on, and saith that towards his latter time, that closeness did impair, and a little perish his understanding. Surely Comineus mought have made the same judgment also, if it had pleased him, of his second master, Lewis the Eleventh, whose closeness was indeed his tormentor. The parable of Pythagoras is dark, but true; Cor ne edito; Eat not the heart. Certainly, if a man would give it a hard phrase, those that want friends, to open themselves unto, are carnnibals of their own hearts. But one thing is most admirable (wherewith I will conclude this first fruit of friendship), which is, that this communicating of a man's self to his friend, works two contrary effects; for it redoubles joys, and cuts griefs in halves. For there is no man, that imparts his joys to his friend, but he joys the more; and no man that imparts his griefs to his friend, but he grieves the less. So that it is in truth, of operation upon a man's mind, of like virtue as the alchemists use to attribute to their stone, for man's body; that it works all contrary effects, but still to the good and benefit of nature. But yet without praying in aid of alchemists, there is a manifest image of this, in the ordinary course of nature. For in bodies, union strengthens and cherishes any natural action; and on the other side, weakens and dulls any violent impression: and even so it is of minds.

The second fruit of friendship, is healthful and sovereign for the understanding, as the first is for the affections. For friendship makes indeed a fair day in the affections, from storm and tempests; but it makes daylight in the understanding, out of darkness, and confusion of thoughts. Neither is this to be understood only of faithful counsel, which a man receives from his friend; but before you come to that, certain it is, that whosoever hath his mind fraught with many thoughts, his wits and understanding do clarify and break up, in the communicating and discoursing with another; he tosses his thoughts more easily; he marshalls them more orderly, he sees how they look when they are turned into words: finally, he waxes wiser than himself; and that more by an hour's discourse, than by a day's meditation. It was well said by Themistocles, to the king of Persia, That speech was like cloth of Arras, opened and put abroad; whereby the imagery doth appear in figure; whereas in thoughts they lie but as in packs. Neither is this second fruit of friendship, in opening the understanding, restrained only to such friends as are able to give a man counsel; (they indeed are best;) but even without that, a man learns of himself, and brings his own thoughts to light, and whets his wits as against a stone, which itself cuts not. In a word, a man were better relate himself to a statua, or picture, than to suffer his thoughts to pass in smother.

Add now, to make this second fruit of friendship complete, that other point, which lies more open, and falls within vulgar observation; which is faithful counsel from a friend. Heraclitus saith well in one of his enigmas, Dry light is ever the best. And certain it is, that the light that a man receives by counsel from another, is drier and purer, than that which comes from his own understanding and judgment; which is ever infused, and drenched, in his affections and customs. So as there is as much difference between the counsel, that a friend gives, and that a man gives himself, as there is between the counsel of a friend, and of a flatterer. For there is no such flatterer as is a man's self; and there is no such remedy against flattery of a man's self, as the liberty of a friend. Counsel is of two sorts: the one concerning manners, the other concerning business. For the first, the best preservative to keep the mind in health, is the faithful admonition of a friend. The calling of a man's self to a strict account, is a medicine, sometime too piercing and corrosive. Reading good books of morality, is a little flat and dead. Observing our faults in others, is sometimes improper for our case. But the best receipt (best, I say, to work, and best to take) is the admonition of a friend. It is a strange thing to behold, what gross errors and extreme absurdities many (especially of the greater sort) do commit, for want of a friend to tell them of them; to the great damage both of their fame and fortune: for, as St. James saith, they are as men that look sometimes into a glass, and presently forget their own shape and favor. As for business, a man may think, if he win, that two eyes see no more than one; or that a gamester sees always more than a looker-on; or that a man in anger, is as wise as he that hath said over the four and twenty letters; or that a musket may be shot off as well upon the arm, as upon a rest; and such other fond and high imaginations, to think himself all in all. But when all is done, the help of good counsel, is that which sets business straight. And if any man think that he will take counsel, but it shall be by pieces; asking counsel in one business, of one man, and in another business, of another man; it is well (that is to say, better, perhaps, than if he asked none at all); but he run two dangers: one, that he shall not be faithfully counselled; for it is a rare thing, except it be from a perfect and entire friend, to have counsel given, but such as shall be bowed and crooked to some ends, which he hath, that gives it. The other, that he shall have counsel given, hurtful and unsafe (though with good meaning), and mixed partly of mischief and partly of remedy; even as if you would call a physician, that is thought good for the cure of the disease you complain of, but is unacquainted with your body; and therefore may put you in way for a present cure, but overthrows your health in some other kind; and so cure the disease, and kill the patient. But a friend that is wholly acquainted with a man's estate, will beware, by furthering any present business, how he dashs upon other inconvenience. And therefore rest not upon scattered counsels; they will rather distract and mislead, than settle and direct.

After these two noble fruits of friendship (peace in the affections, and support of the judgment), follows the last fruit; which is like the pomegranate, full of many kernels; I mean aid, and bearing a part, in all actions and occasions. Here the best way to represent to life the manifold use of friendship, is to cast and see how many things there are, which a man cannot do himself; and then it will appear, that it was a sparing speech of the ancients, to say, that a friend is another himself; for that a friend is far more than himself. Men have their time, and die many times, in desire of some things which they principally take to heart; the bestowing of a child, the finishing of a work, or the like. If a man have a true friend, he may rest almost secure that the care of those things will continue after him. So that a man hath, as it were, two lives in his desires. A man hath a body, and that body is confined to a place; but where friendship is, all offices of life are as it were granted to him, and his deputy. For he may exercise them by his friend. How many things are there which a man cannot, with any face or comeliness, say or do himself? A man can scarce allege his own merits with modesty, much less extol them; a man cannot sometimes brook to supplicate or beg; and a number of the like. But all these things are graceful, in a friend's mouth, which are blushing in a man's own. So again, a man's person hath many proper relations, which he cannot put off. A man cannot speak to his son but as a father; to his wife but as a husband; to his enemy but upon terms: whereas a friend may speak as the case requires, and not as it sorts with the person. But to enumerate these things were endless; I have given the rule, where a man cannot fitly play his own part; if he have not a friend, he may quit the stage.

Moral 13: OF Ambition

AMBITION is like choler; which is an humor that makes men active, earnest, full of alacrity, and stirring, if it be not stopped. But if it be stopped, and cannot have his way, it becomes adust, and thereby malign and venomous. So ambitious men, if they find the way open for their rising, and still get forward, they are rather busy than dangerous; but if they be checked in their desires, they become secretly discontent, and look upon men and matters with an evil eye, and are best pleased, when things go backward; which is the worst property in a servant of a prince, or state. Therefore it is good for princes, if they use ambitious men, to handle it, so as they be still progressive and not retrograde; which, because it cannot be without inconvenience, it is good not to use such natures at all. For if they rise not with their service, they will take order, to make their service fall with them. But since we have said, it were good not to use men of ambitious natures, except it be upon necessity, it is fit we speak, in what cases they are of necessity. Good commanders in the wars must be taken, be they never so ambitious; for the use of their service, dispenses with the rest; and to take a soldier without ambition, is to pull off his spurs. There is also great use of ambitious men, in being screens to princes in matters of danger and envy; for no man will take that part, except he be like a seeled dove, that mounts and mounts, because he cannot see about him. There is use also of ambitious men, in pulling down the greatness of any subject that overtops; as Tiberius used Marco, in the pulling down of Sejanus. Since, therefore, they must be used in such cases, there rests to speak, how they are to be bridled, that they may be less dangerous. There is less danger of them, if they be of mean birth, than if they be noble; and if they be rather harsh of nature, than gracious and popular: and if they be rather new raised, than grown cunning, and fortified, in their greatness. It is counted by some, a weakness in princes, to have favorites; but it is, of all others, the best remedy against ambitious great-ones. For when the way of pleasuring, and displeasuring, lies by the favorite, it is impossible any other should be overgreat. Another means to curb them, is to balance them by others, as proud as they. But then there must be some middle counsellors, to keep things steady; for without that ballast, the ship will roll too much. At the least, a prince may animate and inure some meaner persons, to be as it were scourges, to ambitions men. As for the having of them obnoxious to ruin; if they be of fearful natures, it may do well; but if they be stout and daring, it may precipitate their designs, and prove dangerous. As for the pulling of them down, if the affairs require it, and that it may not be done with safety suddenly, the only way is the interchange, continually, of favors and disgraces; whereby they may not know what to expect, and be, as it were, in a wood. Of ambitions, it is less harmful, the ambition to prevail in great things, than that other, to appear in every thing; for that breeds confusion, and mars business. But yet it is less danger, to have an ambitious man stirring in business, than great in dependences. He that seeks to be eminent amongst able men, hath a great task; but that is ever good for the public. But he, that plots to be the only figure amongst ciphers, is the decay of a whole age. Honor hath three things in it: the vantage ground to do good; the approach to kings and principal persons; and the raising of a man's own fortunes. He that hath the best of these intentions, when he aspires, is an honest man; and that prince, that can discern of these intentions in another that aspires, is a wise prince. Generally, let princes and states choose such ministers, as are more sensible of duty than of using; and such as love business rather upon conscience, than upon bravery, and let them discern a busy nature, from a willing mind.

Moral 14: Of Health

THERE is a wisdom in this; beyond the rules of physic: a man's own observation, what he finds good of, and what he finds hurt of, is the best physic to preserve health. But it is a safer conclusion to say, This agrees not well with me, therefore, I will not continue it; than this, I find no offence of this, therefore I may use it. For strength of nature in youth, passes over many excesses, which are owing a man till his age. Discern of the coming on of years, and think not to do the same things still; for age will not be defied. Beware of sudden change, in any great point of diet, and, if necessity enforce it, fit the rest to it. For it is a secret both in nature and state, that it is safer to change many things, than one. Examine thy customs of diet, sleep, exercise, apparel, and the like; and try, in any thing thou shalt judge hurtful, to discontinue it, by little and little; but so, as if thou dost find any inconvenience by the change, thou come back to it again: for it is hard to distinguish that which is generally held good and wholesome, from that which is good particularly, and fit for thine own body. To be free-minded and cheerfully disposed, at hours of meat, and of sleep, and of exercise, is one of the best precepts of long lasting. As for the passions, and studies of the mind; avoid envy, anxious fears; anger fretting inwards; subtle and knotty inquisitions; joys and exhilarations in excess; sadness not communicated. Entertain hopes; mirth rather than joy; variety of delights, rather than surfeit of them; wonder and admiration, and therefore novelties; studies that fill the mind with splendid and illustrious objects, as histories, fables, and contemplations of nature. If you fly physic in health altogether, it will be too strange for your body, when you shall need it. If you make it too familiar, it will work no extraordinary effect, when sickness comes. I commend rather some diet for certain seasons, than frequent use of physic, except it be grown into a custom. For those diets alter the body more, and trouble it less. Despise no new accident in your body, but ask opinion of it. In sickness, respect health principally; and in health, action. For those that put their bodies to endure in health, may in most sicknesses, which are not very sharp, be cured only with diet, and tendering. Celsus could never have spoken it as a physician, had he not been a wise man withal, when he gives it for one of the great precepts of health and lasting, that a man do vary, and interchange contraries, but with an inclination to the more benign extreme: use fasting and full eating, but rather full eating; watching and sleep, but rather sleep; sitting and exercise, but rather exercise; and the like. So shall nature be cherished, and yet taught masteries. Physicians are, some of them, so pleasing and conformable to the humor of the patient, as they press not the true cure of the disease;

and some other are so regular, in proceeding according to art for the disease, as they respect not sufficiently the condition of the patient. Take one of a middle temper; or if it may not be found in one man, combine two of either sort; and forget not to call as well, the best acquainted with your body, as the best reputed of for his faculty.

Moral 15: OF Riches

I CANNOT call riches better than the baggage of virtue. The Roman word is better, impedimenta. For as the baggage is to an army, so is riches to virtue. It cannot be spared, nor left behind, but it hinders the march; yea, and the care of it, sometimes loses or disturbs the victory. Of great riches there is no real use, except it be in the distribution; the rest is but conceit. So saith Solomon, Where much is, there are many to consume it; and what hath the owner, but the sight of it with his eyes? The personal fruition in any man, cannot reach to feel great riches: there is a custody of them; or a power of dole, and donative of them; or a fame of them; but no solid use to the owner. Do you not see what feigned prices, are set upon little stones and rarities? and what works of ostentation are undertaken, because there might seem to be some use of great riches? But then you will say, they may be of use, to buy men out of dangers or troubles. As Solomon saith, Riches are as a strong hold, in the imagination of the rich man. But this is excellently expressed, that it is in imagination, and not always in fact. For certainly great riches, have sold more men, than they have bought out. Seek not proud riches, but such as thou mayest get justly, use soberly, distribute cheerfully, and leave contentedly. Yet have no abstract nor friarly contempt of them. But distinguish, as Cicero saith well of Rabirius Posthumus, In studio rei amplificandae apparebat, non avaritiae praedam, sed instrumentum bonitati quaeri. Harken also to Solomon, and beware of hasty gathering of riches; Qui festinat ad divitias, non erit insons. The poets feign, that when Plutus (which is Riches) is sent from Jupiter, he limps and goes slowly; but when he is sent from Pluto, he runs, and is swift of foot. Meaning that riches gotten by good means, and just labor, pace slowly; but when they come by the death of others (as by the course of inheritance, testaments, and the like), they come tumbling upon a man. But it mought be applied likewise to Pluto, taking him for the devil. For when riches come from the devil (as by fraud and oppression, and unjust means), they come upon speed. The ways to enrich are many, and most of them foul. Parsimony is one of the best, and yet is not innocent; for it withholds men from works of liberality and charity. The improvement of the ground, is the most natural obtaining of riches; for it is our great mother's blessing, the earth's; but it is slow. And yet where men of great wealth do stoop to husbandry, it multiplies riches exceedingly. I knew a nobleman in England, that had the greatest audits of any man in my time; a great grazier, a great sheep-master, a great timber man, a great collier, a great corn-master, a great lead-man, and so of iron, and a number of the like points of husbandry. So as the earth seemed a sea to him, in respect of the perpetual importation. It was truly observed by one, that himself came very hardly, to a little riches, and very easily, to great riches. For when a man's stock is come to that, that he can expect the prime of markets, and overcome those bargains, which for their greatness are few men's money, and be partner in the industries of younger men, he cannot but increase mainly. The gains of ordinary trades and vocations are honest; and furthered by two things chiefly: by diligence, and by a good name, for good and fair dealing. But the gains of bargains, are of a more doubtful nature; when men shall wait upon others' necessity, broke by servants and instruments to draw them on, put off others cunningly, that would be better chapmen, and the like practices, which are crafty and naught. As for the chopping of bargains, when a man buys not to hold but to sell over again, that commonly grinds double, both upon the seller, and upon the buyer. Sharings do greatly enrich, if the hands be well chosen, that are trusted. Usury is the certainest means of gain, though one of the worst; as that whereby a man doth eat his bread, in sudore vultus alieni; and besides, doth plough upon Sundays. But yet certain though it be, it hath flaws; for that the scriveners and brokers do value unsound men, to serve their own turn. The fortune in being the first, in an invention or in a privilege, doth cause sometimes a wonderful overgrowth in riches; as it was with the first sugar man, in the Canaries. Therefore if a man can play the true logician, to have as well judgment, as invention, he may do great matters; especially if the times be fit. He that rests upon gains certain, shall hardly grow to great riches; and he that puts all upon adventures, doth oftentimes break and come to poverty: it is good, therefore, to guard adventures with certainties, that may uphold losses. Monopolies, and coemption of wares for re-sale, where they are not restrained, are great means to enrich; especially if the party have intelligence, what things are like to come into request, and so store himself beforehand. Riches gotten by service, though it be of the best rise, yet when they are gotten by flattery, feeding humors, and other servile conditions, they may be placed amongst the worst. As for fishing for testaments and executorships (as Tacitus saith of Seneca, testamenta et orbos tamquam indagine capi), it is yet worse; by how much men submit themselves to meaner persons, than in service. Believe not much, them that seem to despise riches; for they despise them, that despair of them; and none worse, when they come to them. Be not penny-wise; riches have wings, and sometimes they fly away of themselves, sometimes they must be set flying, to bring in more. Men leave their riches, either to their kindred, or to the public; and moderate portions, prosper best in both. A great state left to an heir, is as a lure to all the birds of prey round about, to seize on him, if he be not the better stablished in years and judgment. Likewise glorious gifts and foundations, are like sacrifices without salt; and but the painted sepulchres of alms, which soon will putrefy, and corrupt inwardly. Therefore measure not thine advancements, by quantity, but frame them by measure: and defer not charities till death; for, certainly, if a man weigh it rightly, he that doth so, is rather liberal of another man's, than of his own.

Moral 16: Of Nobility

WE WILL speak of nobility, first as a portion of an estate, then as a condition of particular persons. A monarchy, where there is no nobility at all, is ever a pure and absolute tyranny; as that of the Turks. For nobility attempers sovereignty, and draws the eyes of the people, somewhat aside from the line royal. But for democracies, they need it not; and they are commonly more quiet, and less subject to sedition, than where there are stirps of nobles. For men's eyes are upon the business, and not upon the persons; or if upon the persons, it is for the business' sake, as fittest, and not for flags and pedigree. We see the Switzers last well, notwithstanding their diversity of religion, and of cantons. For utility is their bond, and not respects. The united provinces of the Low Countries, in their government, excel; for where there is an equality, the consultations are more indifferent, and the payments and tributes, more cheerful. A great and potent nobility, adds majesty to a monarch, but diminishs power; and putts life and spirit into the people, but presses their fortune. It is well, when nobles are not too great for sovereignty nor for justice; and yet maintained in that height, as the insolency of inferiors may be broken upon them, before it come on too fast upon the majesty of kings. A numerous nobility causes poverty, and inconvenience in a state; for it is a surcharge of expense; and besides, it being of necessity, that many of the nobility fall, in time, to be weak in fortune, it makes a kind of disproportion, between honor and means.

As for nobility in particular persons; it is a reverend thing, to see an ancient castle or building, not in decay; or to see a fair timber tree, sound and perfect. How much more, to behold an ancient noble family, which has stood against the waves and weathers of time! For new nobility is but the act of power, but ancient nobility is the act of time. Those that are first raised to nobility, are commonly more virtuous, but less innocent, than their descendants; for there is rarely any rising, but by a commixture of good and evil arts. But it is reason, the memory of their virtues remain to their posterity, and their faults die with themselves. Nobility of birth commonly abates industry; and he that is not industrious, envies him that is. Besides, noble persons cannot go much higher; and he that stands at a stay, when others rise, can hardly avoid motions of envy. On the other side, nobility extinguishs the passive envy from others, towards them; because they are in possession of honor. Certainly, kings that have able men of their nobility, shall find ease in employing them, and a better slide into their business; for people naturally bend to them, as born in some sort to command.

.

Moral 17: Of Beauty

VIRTUE is like a rich stone, best plain set; and surely virtue is best, in a body that is comely, though not of delicate features; and that hath rather dignity of presence, than beauty of aspect. Neither is it almost seen, that very beautiful persons are otherwise of great virtue; as if nature were rather busy, not to err, than in labor to produce excellency. And therefore they prove accomplished, but not of great spirit; and study rather behavior, than virtue. But this holds not always: for Augustus Caesar, Titus Vespasianus, Philip le Belle of France, Edward the Fourth of England, Alcibiades of Athens, Ismael the Sophy of Persia, were all high and great spirits; and yet the most beautiful men of their times. In beauty, that of favor, is more than that of color; and that of decent and gracious motion, more than that of favor. That is the best part of beauty, which a picture cannot express; no, nor the first sight of the life. There is no excellent beauty, that hath not some strangeness in the proportion. A man cannot tell whether Apelles, or Albert Durer, were the more trifler; whereof the one, would make a personage by geometrical proportions; the other, by taking the best parts out of divers faces, to make one excellent. Such personages, I think, would please nobody, but the painter that made them. Not but I think a painter may make a better face than ever was; but he must do it by a kind of felicity (as a musician that makes an excellent air in music), and not by rule. A man shall see faces, that if you examine them part by part, you shall find never a good; and yet altogether do well. If it be true that the principal part of beauty is in decent motion, certainly it is no marvel, though persons in years seem many times more amiable; pulchrorum autumnus pulcher; for no youth can be comely but by pardon, and considering the youth, as to make up the comeliness. Beauty is as summer fruits,) which are easy to corrupt, and cannot last; and for the most part it makes a dissolute youth, and an age a little out of countenance; but yet certainly again, if it light well, it makes virtue shine, and vices blush.

Moral 18: Of Goodness

I TAKE goodness in this sense, the affecting of the weal of men, which is that the Grecians call philanthropia; and the word humanity (as it is used) is a little too light to express it. Goodness I call the habit, and goodness of nature, the inclination. This of all virtues, and dignities of the mind, is the greatest; being the character of the Deity: and without it, man is a busy, mischievous, wretched thing; no better than a kind of vermin. Goodness answers to the theological virtue, charity, and admits no excess, but error. The desire of power in excess, caused the angels to fall; the desire of knowledge in excess, caused man to fall: but in charity there is no excess; neither can angel, nor man, come in dan ger by it. The inclination to goodness, is imprinted deeply in the nature of man; insomuch, that if it issue not towards men, it will take unto other living creatures; as it is seen in the Turks, a cruel people, who nevertheless are kind to beasts, and give alms, to dogs and birds; insomuch, as Busbechius reports, a Christian boy, in Constantinople, had like to have been stoned, for gagging in a waggishness a long-billed fowl. Errors indeed in this virtue of goodness, or charity, may be committed. The Italians have an ungracious proverb, Tanto buon che val niente: so good, that he is good for nothing. And one of the doctors of Italy, Nicholas Machiavel, had the confidence to put in writing, almost in plain terms, That the Christian faith, had given up good men, in prey to those that are tyrannical and unjust. Which he spake, because indeed there was never law, or sect, or opinion, did so much magnify goodness, as the Christian religion doth. Therefore, to avoid the scandal and the danger both, it is good, to take knowledge of the errors of an habit so excellent. Seek the good of other men, but be not in bondage to their faces or fancies; for that is but facility, or softness; which takes an honest mind prisoner. Neither give thou AEsop's cock a gem, who would be better pleased, and happier, if he had had a barley-corn. The example of God, teaches the lesson truly: He sends his rain, and makes his sun to shine, upon the just and unjust; but he doth not rain wealth, nor shine honor and virtues, upon men equally. Common benefits, are to be communicate with all; but peculiar benefits, with choice. And beware how in making the portraiture, thou breakest the pattern. For divinity, makes the love of ourselves the pattern; the love of our neighbors, but the portraiture. Sell all thou hast, and give it to the poor, and follow me: but, sell not all thou hast, except thou come and follow me; that is, except thou have a vocation, wherein thou mayest do as much good, with little means as with great; for otherwise, in feeding the streams, thou driest the fountain. Neither is there only a habit of goodness, directed by right reason; but there is in some men, even in nature, a disposition towards it; as on the other side, there is a natural malignity. For there be, that in their nature do not affect the good of others. The lighter sort of malignity, turns but to a crassness, or frowardness, or aptness to oppose, or difficulties, or the like; but the deeper sort, to envy and mere mischief. Such men, in other men's calamities, are, as it were, in season, and are ever on the loading part: not so good as the dogs, that licked Lazarus' sores; but like flies, that are still buzzing upon any thing that is raw; misanthropi, that make it their practice, to bring men to the bough, and yet never a tree for the purpose in their gardens, as Timon had. Such dispositions, are the very errors of human nature; and yet they are the fittest timber, to make great politics of; like to knee timber, that is good for ships, that are ordained to be tossed; but not for building houses, that shall stand firm. The parts and signs of goodness, are many. If a man be gracious and courteous to strangers, it shows he is a citizen of the world, and that his heart is no island, cut off from other lands, but a continent, that joins to them. If he be compassionate towards the afflictions of others, it shows that his heart is like the noble tree, that is wounded itself, when it gives the balm. If he easily pardons, and remits offences, it shows that his mind is planted above injuries; so that he cannot be shot. If he be thankful for small benefits, it shows that he weighs men's minds, and not their trash. But above all, if he have St. Paul's perfection, that he would wish to be anathema from Christ, for the salvation of his brethren, it shows much of a divine nature, and a kind of conformity with Christ himself.

Moral 19: Of Parents

AND CHILDREN

THE joys of parents are secret; and so are their griefs and fears. They cannot utter the one; nor they will not utter the other. Children sweeten labors; but they make misfortunes more bitter. They increase the cares of life; but they mitigate the remembrance of death. The perpetuity by generation is common to beasts; but memory, merit, and noble works, are proper to men. And surely a man shall see the noblest works and foundations have proceeded from childless men; which have sought to express the images of their minds, where those of their bodies have failed. So the care of posterity is most in them, that have no posterity. They that are the first raisers of their houses, are most indulgent towards their children; beholding them as the continuance, not only of their kind, but of their work; and so both children and creatures.

The difference in affection, of parents towards their several children, is many times unequal; and sometimes unworthy; especially in the mothers; as Solomon saith, A wise son rejoices the father, but an ungracious son shames the mother. A man shall see, where there is a house full of children, one or two of the eldest respected, and the youngest made wantons; but in the midst, some that are as it were forgotten, who many times, nevertheless, prove the best. The illiberality of parents, in allowance towards their children, is an harmful error; makes them base; acquaints them with shifts; makes them sort with mean company; and makes them surfeit more when they come to plenty. And therefore the proof is best, when men keep their authority towards the children, but not their purse. Men have a foolish manner (both parents and schoolmasters and servants) in creating and breeding an emulation between brothers, during childhood, which many times sorts to discord when they are men, and disturbs families. The Italians make little difference between children, and nephews or near kinsfolks; but so they be of the lump, they care not though they pass not through their own body. And, to say truth, in nature it is much a like matter; insomuch that we see a nephew sometimes resembles an uncle, or a kinsman, more than his own parent; as the blood happens. Let parents choose betimes, the vocations and courses they mean their children should take; for then they are most flexible; and let them not too much apply themselves to the disposition of their children, as thinking they will take best to that, which they have most mind to. It is true, that if the affection or aptness of the children be extraordinary, then it is good not to cross it; but generally the precept is good, optimum elige, suave et facile illud faciet consuetudo. Younger brothers are commonly fortunate, but seldom or never where the elder are disinherited.

Moral 20: Of Marriage

AND SINGLE LIFE

HE THAT hath wife and children hath given hostages to fortune; for they are impediments to great enterprises, either of virtue or mischief. Certainly the best works, and of greatest merit for the public, have proceeded from the unmarried or childless men; which both in affection and means, have married and endowed the public. Yet it were great reason that those that have children, should have greatest care of future times; unto which they know they must transmit their dearest pledges. Some there are, who though they lead a single life, yet their thoughts do end with themselves, and account future times impertinences. Nay, there are some other, that account wife and children, but as bills of charges. Nay more, there are some foolish rich covetous men, that take a pride, in having no children, because they may be thought so much the richer. For perhaps they have heard some talk, Such an one is a great rich man, and another except to it, Yea, but he hath a great charge of children; as if it were an abatement to his riches. But the most ordinary cause of a single life, is liberty, especially in certain self-pleasing and humorous minds, which are so sensible of every restraint, as they will go near to think their girdles and garters, to be bonds and shackles. Unmarried men are best friends, best masters, best servants; but not always best subjects; for they are light to run away; and almost all fugitives, are of that condition. A single life doth well with churchmen; for charity will hardly water the ground, where it must first fill a pool. It is indifferent for judges and magistrates; for if they be facile and corrupt, you shall have a servant, five times worse than a wife. For soldiers, I find the generals commonly in their hortatives, put men in mind of their wives and children; and I think the despising of marriage amongst the Turks, maketh the vulgar soldier more base. Certainly wife and children are a kind of discipline of humanity; and single men, though they may be many times more charitable, because their means are less exhaust, yet, on the other side, they are more cruel and hardhearted (good to make severe inquisitors), because their tenderness is not so oft called upon. Grave natures, led by custom, and therefore constant, are commonly loving husbands, as was said of Ulysses, vetulam suam praetulit immortalitati. Chaste women are often proud and froward, as presuming upon the merit of their chastity. It is one of the best bonds, both of chastity and obedience, in the wife, if she think her husband wise; which she will never do, if she find him jealous. Wives are young men's mistresses; companions for middle age; and old men's nurses. So as a man may have a quarrel to marry, when he will. But yet he was reputed one of the wise men, that made answer to the question, when a man should marry, - A young man not yet, an elder man not at all. It is often seen that bad husbands, have very good wives; whether it be, that it raises the price of their husband's kindness, when it comes; or that the wives take a pride in their patience. But this never fails, if the bad husbands were of their own choosing, against their friends' consent; for then they will be sure to make good their own folly.

Moral 21: Of Nature

IN MEN

NATURE is often hidden; sometimes overcome; seldom extinguished. Force, makes nature more violent in the return; doctrine and discourse, makes nature less importune; but custom only doth alter and subdue nature. He that seeks victory over his nature, let him not set himself too great, nor too small tasks; for the first will make him dejected by often failings; and the second will make him a small proceeder, though by often prevailings. And at the first let him practise with helps, as swimmers do with bladders or rushes; but after a time let him practise with disadvantages, as dancers do with thick shoes. For it breeds great perfection, if the practice be harder than the use. Where nature is mighty, and therefore the victory hard, the degrees had need be, first to stay and arrest nature in time; like to him that would say over the four and twenty letters when he was angry; then to go less in quantity; as if one should, in forbearing wine, come from drinking healths, to a draught at a meal; and lastly, to discontinue altogether. But if a man have the fortitude, and resolution, to enfranchise himself at once, that is the best:

Optimus ille animi vindex laedentia pectus Vincula qui rupit, dedoluitque semel.

Neither is the ancient rule amiss, to bend nature, as a wand, to a contrary extreme, whereby to set it right, understanding it, where the contrary extreme is no vice. Let not a man force a habit upon himself, with a perpetual continuance, but with some intermission. For both the pause reinforces the new onset; and if a man that is not perfect, be ever in practice, he shall as well practise his errors, as his abilities, and induce one habit of both; and there is no means to help this, but by seasonable intermissions. But let not a man trust his victory over his nature, too far; for nature will lay buried a great time, and yet revive, upon the occasion or temptation. Like as it was with AEsop's damsel, turned from a cat to a woman, who sat very demutely at the board's end, till a mouse ran before her. Therefore, let a man either avoid the occasion altogether; or put himself often to it, that he may be little moved with it. A man's nature is best perceived in privateness, for there is no affectation; in passion, for that puttes a man out of his precepts; and in a new case or experiment, for there custom leaves him. They are happy men, whose natures sort with their vocations; otherwise they may say, multum incola fuit anima mea; when they converse in those things, they do not affect. In studies, whatsoever a man commands upon himself, let him set hours for it; but whatsoever is agreeable to his nature, let him take no care for any set times; for his thoughts will fly to it, of themselves; so as the spaces of other business, or studies, will suffice. A man's nature, runs either to herbs or weeds; therefore let him seasonably water the one, and destroy the other.

[This essay is a condensed version of the original bacon essays with only the mos essential morals]

A Glossary OF ARCHAIC WORDS AND PHRASES

Abridgment: miniature

Absurd: stupid, unpolished

Abuse: cheat, deceive

Aculeate: stinging

Adamant: loadstone

Adust: scorched

Advoutress: adulteress

Affect: like, desire

Antic: clown

Appose: question

Arietation: battering-ram

Audit: revenue

Avoidance: secret outlet

Battle: battalion

Bestow: settle in life

Blanch: flatter, evade

Brave: boastful

Bravery: boast, ostentation

Broke: deal in brokerage

Broken: shine by comparison

Broken music: part music

Cabinet: secret

Calendar: weather forecast

Card: chart, map

Care not to: are reckless

Cast: plan

Cat: cate, cake

Charge and adventure: cost and risk

Check with: interfere

Chop: bandy words

Civil: peaceful

Close: secret, secretive

Collect: infer

Compound: compromise

Consent: agreement

Curious: elaborate

Custom: import duties

Deceive: rob

Derive: divert

Difficileness: moroseness

Discover: reveal

Donative: money gift

Doubt: fear

Equipollent: equally powerful

Espial: spy

Estate: state

Facility: of easy persuasion

Fair: rather

Fame: rumor

Favor: feature

Flashy: insipid

Foot-pace: lobby

Foreseen: guarded against

Froward: stubborn

Futile: babbling

Globe: complete body

Glorious: showy, boastful

Humorous: capricious

Hundred poll: hundredth head

Impertinent: irrelevant

Implicit: entangled

In a mean: in moderation

In smother: suppressed

Indifferent: impartial

Intend: attend to

Knap:knoll

Leese: lose

Let: hinder

Loose: shot

Lot: spell

Lurch: intercept

Make: profit, get

Manage: train

Mate: conquer

Material: business-like

Mere-stone: boundary stone

Muniting: fortifying

Nerve: sinew

Obnoxious: subservient, liable

Oes: round spangles

Pair: impair

Pardon: allowance

Passable: mediocre

Pine-apple-tree: pine

Plantation: colony

Platform: plan

Plausible: praiseworthy

Point device: excessively precise

Politic: politician

Poll: extort

Poser: examiner

Practice: plotting

Preoccupate: anticipate

Prest: prepared

Prick: plant

Proper: personal

Prospective: stereoscope

Proyne: prune

Purprise: enclosure

Push: pimple

Quarrel: pretext

Quech: flinch

Reason: principle

Recamera: retiring-room

Return: reaction

Return: wing running back

Rise: dignity

Round: straight

Save: account for

Scantling: measure

Seel: blind

Shrewd: mischievous

Sort: associate

Spial: spy

Staddle: sapling

Steal: do secretly

Stirp: family

Stond: stop, stand

Stoved: hot-housed

Style: title

Success: outcome

Sumptuary law: law against

extravagance

Superior globe: the heavens

Temper: proportion

Tendering: nursing

Tract: line, trait

Travel: travail, labor

Treaties: treatises

Trench to: touch

Trivial: common

Turquet: Turkish dwarf

Under foot: below value

Unready: untrained

Usury: interest

Value: certify

Virtuous: able

Votary: vowed

Wanton: spoiled

Wood: maze

Work: manage, utilize

(End Of Story)